A TASTING PARTY

Library of Congress Cataloging-in-Publication Data
Moncure, Jane Belk.
A tasting party / Jane Belk-Moncure;
illustrated by Viki Woodworth.
p. cm.
Summary: Flowers, leaves, seeds, roots, fruits, dairy
foods, and meats are sampled at different
types of food tasting parties.
ISBN 1-56766-283-8

1. Taste — Juvenile literature. [1. Taste.] I. Title.

QP456.M66 1997   97-6267
612.8'7 — dc21   CIP
                                                      AC

BY JANE BELK-MONCURE / ILLUSTRATED BY VIKI WOODWORTH

A TASTING PARTY

Click-clack down the track,
a train is coming to town.

"It is time for a party. Come take a ride,"
says a funny clown. "Just step inside."

A tasting party is so much fun with animal friends in Car Number One.

Take a seat with a pony,
a hen, and two goats.
They are tasting corn,
wheat, and oats.

You can taste cereal,
muffins, and rice.
Noodles and bagels
are very nice.

Try hot
popcorn for a treat.
Is it salty? Sour? Bitter? Or sweet?

Foods made with whole
grains help you grow strong
so you will have energy all day long.

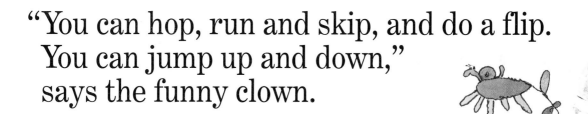

"You can hop, run and skip, and do a flip.
You can jump up and down,"
says the funny clown.

Let's skip along
to Car Number Two.

"More animal friends
will taste foods
with you.

Come in," says a friendly kangaroo.
Fruits and veggies give you energy , too.

Taste veggies with the rabbit,
and fruit with the baby bears.

Monkeys will share some oranges,
bananas, grapes, and pears.

Pass the flowers. Pass the roots.
We love veggies. We love fruits.

Clown says, "Come along. Hop with me.
Let's taste foods in Car Number Three."

"Come in," says the cow. "Step this way.
Today is dairy food tasting day."

"We have yogurt, milk,
and cheese for you,"
say a kitten, a lamb,
and a puppy dog, too.

"I do love cheese," says a
    dressed-up mouse.
"We have all kinds of yummy
    cheese at our house."

"Dairy foods help our bones grow strong," says a puppy.

"That's why we can play all day long."

"How about some ice cream for a treat," says the clown.

Is it salty? Bitter? Sour? Or sweet?

Now let's run to
Car Number Four.
"Come in," says a dressed-up
squirrel at the door.

"Taste sunflower seeds with the chipmunks.
Taste nuts with the cockatoo.
Have some peanuts,"
says the elephant from the city zoo.

"Here's a picnic basket," says the clown, "with more good food for you.
   We will stop at the park so your friends can have a tasting party, too."

"Have a tasting party every day.
Try different foods," the animals say,
as the little train chugs away.
Toot. Toot. Toot.